Mumbai Postcards

Notes to a Grandson

દહેજ
दहेज
Dahej
392130
भारतीय डाक
India Post

Mumbai Postcards

Notes to a Grandson

HARSHA V. DEHEJIA

Motilal Banarsidass Publications

MOTILAL BANARSIDASS
PUBLICATIONS

4741/23, Ansari Road, Daryaganj, New Delhi - 110002 (India)
Email: mlbd@mlbd.com | sales@mlbd.com | exports@mlbd.com
Website: www.mlbd.com

Mumbai Postcards

by

Harsha V. Dehejia

First Edition Published in 2024

Published in India by Motilal Banarsidass Publications

ISBN : 978-81-96165-36-9 (PB)

Printed and bound in India

Credits

TEXT
©Harsha V. Dehejia

PHOTOS
Mohammed Rafique Khan | Mukesh Yadav | Vinod Contractor | Harsha V. Dehejia

DESIGN
Shrinidhi Sridhar

Dedicated to our grandson Manu

and to all the Manus

who spend their lives under a Oak tree but

who may want to seek the roots of their ancestral Pipal tree.

LET US BEGIN

I have always been fascinated by Indian postcards. In such a small space there is so much you can write, and for a fraction of a rupee. After you have dropped it off in some of the most unpretentious post boxes, it reaches the recipient in a few days. After spending sixty years in the modern Western civilization, I felt I was ready to make a bird's eye view comparison of that civilization with that of my ancestral Indian civilisation. Civilization is a broad umbrella term and can include a number of features, some of which may be unimportant for our purpose, like wars and conquests, politics and economics, sociology and demographics. We are interested in those values that inform human behavior, like ethics and compassion, art and craft.

Even more we are interested in metaphysical values of the civilisation, their concept of space and time, their expression of what is enduring and beautiful, their humanitarian values, their concept of what is permanent and what is evanescent. In other words our quest is of knowledge in India and in the West. The arts are always a mirror of any civilization and will reveal some underlying values and concepts of the sacred and the divine.

In reading these postcards you might ask me, "I am happy, peaceful and successful in the life that I am leading, whether I am in in India or in the West. Why then should I explore Hindu thought?" That is a valid question. I am not recommending that you explore Hindu thought as an expedient or a means of bringing relief or solace from suffering, or even as an insurance for future problems in life. Saying that would be to downgrade the majesty, depth and grandeur of Hindu thought. I will admit however that some people who have become dropouts of life, for a variety of reasons, do turn to India, lie on its beaches, go to gurus, smoke pot and claim that they are turning to Hinduism. This is a caricature of Hinduism. Hindu thought is a celebration of beauty and cosmic order in the universe and our place in it, our earliest *rishis* or seers, were poets of beauty, they had the courage to accept that there was a beautiful mystery in the world and even the gods did not know how creation took place, there was a sense of wonder within them as they looked at the sky filled with the colours of dawn in the morning and stars at night, they measured their lives with the movement of the sun and created time with the phases of the moon, they accepted that language was limited and finite but even then they could realise the infinite within the spaces of their mind and they declared that they have known this mystery of life radiant as the sun, they had no sense of defeat; they had not committed any sin, they were not beaten down with suffering either their own or in the world around, they were not on their supplicant knees but instead stood firmly on this earth even as they raised their hands to the heavens above, they did not have to accept any commandments or dictates of prophets or the son of god, but felt that the highest truth was within them which they had to discover, and as they did this they would go from joy to greater joy for that, is the essence of life and Hindu living. Tagore was right in saying that he was a poet and that his religion was the search and celebration of beauty and he wrote that *ananda loke, mangala loke satya sundaro birajo*, that the truth of the world resides in the world of the auspicious and the blissful. It is this world that I am asking you to explore and enjoy.

In this globalised world one hears that a New Yorker is no different from a Mumbaikar. This is true only up to a point. To stop here would be to succumb to an anthropologic view of the world. Even when the *achar* (behavior), *vichar* (thinking) and *ahar* (cuisine and costume) in a globalized world are similar from New York to Nagpur and London to Lucknow, but their concept of what is ultimately real or Truth is significantly different, and it is this difference that we are trying to explore. This exploration does not require you to give up anything or deny anything, it just may open up a new window for you, it might admit more light into your mind and make it more effulgent, it could brings a new fragrance and a charged aesthetic sensibility, and perhaps, foster a joyous view of life and more holistic living. Try it!

A few words about the Indian psyche. The Indian psyche which is a product of a predominantly *krishi sanskriti* or agricultural culture, responds culturally and aesthetically to the luxurious and fecund Indian environment, full of lush trees and green foliage, the radiant sun and a clear and starry sky, fragrant blossoms and winding creepers, the colour and the radiance of everything that grows, and all of this is reflected in the many motifs that are represented in a variety of beautiful representations. The word *krishi* arises from the root *krs* which means both *akarshana* or attraction and *vilekhana* or ploughing. In depicting this through *akritis* or the various forms the artisan and the housewife, the poet and the potter, are expressing their *akarshana* or attraction and captivation of the beautiful *prakriti* or nature all around them, it is an affirmation of growth and rejoicing of life in its manifold forms, a veneration and recognition of abundance and fullness as an integral part of life and living and it is that they represent and recreate in their artistic representations and surround their lived lives with it. This growth and fertility which the Indian psyche venerates has many nuances of meanings. Growth implies not only material or physical growth but even more importantly, it points to emotional and spiritual growth and fulfilment.

Bharatiya sanskriti or Indian culture revels and luxuriates in concepts and representations of abundance and prosperity, the lushness of vegetation, the ripening of what is planted in the field, majestic trees that arise from the soil and rise to touch the sky, whispering rivers and rushing brooks, tranquil lakes and roaring waterfalls, life giving rain and nourishing sunlight, all of which create a verdant, embracing and luxuriant landscape. It is this landscape that shapes our habits and habitats, our minds and hearts, our rites and rituals, our sacraments and seasonal celebrations, our fairs and festivals, and above all our religious and philosophic view of the world and our own concepts of *moksha* or ultimate freedom and realisation.

This is in sharp contrast to the arid environment of the desert where the Judeo-Christian traditions were born and which informs the modern West. It is in the fitness of things that our artistic representations arise from this bedrock of the celebration of growth and fecundity and speaks so eloquently of a *krishi sanskriti*. Most of the motifs of lengthy are vegetative, like the *kalpavriksha* or wish fulfilling tree and the *padma* or the lotus, the mango and the *lata* or the vine, the Banana tree and the Pipal tree. We also incorporate the peacock and the parrot, the fish and the snake. An important part of the adornment is also the *kalasha* or the ritual water pot. These are auspicious symbols for us, *mangalmaya*, denoting growth and fertility, fecundity and prosperity, bestowing grace and auspiciousness and above all suggesting *purnatva* or fullness and completeness and wholesomeness of life and living. There is in this a life affirming world view, of joyous and radiant engagement with the world, of a desire to make this life beautiful and meaningful, of fostering and celebrating *pravritti* or growth and not *nivritti* or retirement, of giving expression to *kamana* or desire and making it an essential and joyous part of life. Growth and fertility at one level mean physical and biologic growth but at another level it also refers to emotional and spiritual enhancement. Whether it is just a lotus or a *kalpavriksha*, there is in that motif a cosmic view, for both go from the nether worlds to the heavens, from *bhumi* to *gagan*, earth to sky, and encompass and include everything in between.

In this essay, in the form of postcards, I am writing to Manu in a conversational style, my grandson, who lives far away from me. I also include all the Manus of the world who find themselves of Indian origin but not living in India and who sometime in their lives are bound to seek their roots, and compare it with the tree under which they live, that has grown away from India, in the West. Other than my ancestral Indian civilization, I have lived and worked in England, the U.S A. and Canada. This is what I call the modern West. The West, it is said, is that necessary evil which we Indians must understand and live with, without losing ourselves entirely in its iron embrace.

I am not an academic of modern Western thought and nor do I make the claim that I have read its weighty tomes. However, having interacted with patients and students for sixty years, and this has helped me touch their lives quite deeply, I have come to understand the modern Western civilization through them. You might say that this is anecdotal. Perhaps it is, but simple conversations with my patients and students, conversations at the water cooler in corridors of Universities with colleagues, lengthy discussions over a cup of tea with colleagues who have spent time in India and understand the Indian civilisation, and many contemplative moments spent under a Maple tree and watch the world go by, has given me an insight into the modern Western civilisation, which though not academic and peer reviewed, is nonetheless significant.

This is the first of a series of what I have called Mumbai postcards. Read them at your leisure. I will keep them short, but hopefully they are seminal and could lead to a healthy discussion and introspection on your part.

They stem basically from my spending more than half a century in the modern Western civilization, and even though acknowledging the benefits of that civilization, I have discovered serious fault lines in that.

These postcards are intended for the young people of our times, both Western and Indian, as in a globalised world, the young people of urban India are no different from those in the West. For Indian youths in India this is an opportunity to explore and refresh your traditional wisdom, and for Indian youths in the West, this is an invitation for homecoming, to know your roots and nourish them.

Welcome.

Let me start with the Pandemic. There is distinctly less fear and anxiety about the Pandemic in Mumbai as compared to Ottawa. I am not prepared to accept that Mumbaikars are foolhardy or reckless, although that may play a small part. I feel that we in India derive a lot of strength from people around us, be they family, neighbours, co-workers, domestic helpers and even strangers. I feel that the ancient adage, *vasudhaiva kutumabakam*, the world is a family, is not just an empty slogan but people of all walks of life believe in it. Secondly, Indians have greater spiritual resources than the average person in the West. While the simple man on the street in Mumbai will point a finger to the sky assuring himself of divine protection, the more sophisticated Indian has a more nuanced spiritual strength. I find this refreshingly different from the fearful and fear-mongering ethos of the Western world. The intellect driven, science oriented West has opened itself into a lot of weaknesses. We in ancient India did make some significant scientific discoveries, like the zero in mathematics or a knowledge of the cosmos even without a telescope. However, our science was always tied to spirituality. In the West science becomes technology.

Let me give you an example of how Indian science and spirituality go together. When in 2021, The Indian Space Research Organisation was sending an unmanned rocket to the moon, they first performed a *puja*, a religious ceremony, to ensure success. The fact that the mission failed is besides the point, but our scientists did not rely only on science but had equal faith in powers spiritual for the success of the mission. I know a Indian cardiac surgeon who reads the Bhagavad Gita before commencing cardiac surgery. I know a Indian Pediatrician who has a picture of his chosen god on his desk and asks for his blessings even as he treats his patients. Most Indian cars have a small religious shrine on their dashboard from whom they seek religious blessings in their travel. Some small examples of how we do not divorce science from spirituality.

It was a busy day in my medical office in Ottawa, phones were ringing, the waiting room was full and I was a bit behind schedule. As I was racing through the office my eyes fell on a small icon of the Nataraja that I had on the window sill. The money plant next to it grew, and passed through the Nataraja, and came out. I got so excited and called everyone and told them that the plant was venerating the Nataraja. To which my nurses and secretaries said that the plant was overgrown and they took a scissors and cut it. To my Indian *drishti*, world view, the sap that flows through the plants is the same *rasa* that animates us and it is thus that I have a living connection with them and they with me. This enriches my life and widens my awareness of myself and the world around me. In not subscribing to this view, my Canadian brothers and sisters make their world homocentric and self-centred.

As I write this in the summer of 2023 Canada's much beloved health care system is in a crisis: waiting lists for procedures and elective surgery are several months long, wait times at the Emergency are 15-18 hours, ambulance response time can be up to1 hour. Social services to the elderly and the disadvantaged are dwindling. Senior citizens, particularly if they are mentally challenged, are being abandoned by their families and put in pigeon-hole senior homes. All of this and more is very disheartening. Canadians want their government to solve all their problems. This is what happens in a socialistic society. Why don't they take a page from India? Traditional Indian society is built upon multi-generational living and the building of communities. When father and son live in the same home, albeit in separate quarters, it is a win win situation for both. The elderly parents do not suffer loneliness and alienation and the younger do not have to worry about babysitting. We in the West make friends, but this is not the same as building communities. In a community there is communal living, which while taking away the much prized privacy, creates a web of connections. Sooner or later, Canada and the modern West will have to follow the Indian example.

डाकघर
POST OFFICE
इंडिया पोस्ट पेमेन्ट्स बैंक
हिक्किम शाखा डाकघर
हिक्किम
HIKKIM
Branch Post Office
Pin Code:-
172114
Working Hours:-
भारतीय डाक
India Post
"विश्व का सबसे ऊँचाई पर स्थित डाकघर"
"THE WORLD'S HIGHEST POST OFFICE"
HEIGHT ऊँचाई 4440 Mts. मी॰ {14567 Ft. फीट}
LETTER BOX
INDIA POST
NEXT CLEARANCE

On January 10, 2022 the Museum in Mumbai (CSMVS as it called) celebrated its centenary. It was built during the hey day of the British *raj* and like other museums in Europe it was a Western construct. The concept of a Museum was alien to the Indian mind. We had temples, rock cut caves and *chitrashalas,* picture galleries in palaces where forms and figures were beautifully carved and painted, stories were told on the wall and even though they were religiously venerated, they had a strong aesthetic appeal. We in present-day India have many Museums, but it behooves us to have an Indian eye as we visit these Museums. That Indian eye does not just see but perceives, it is synaesthetic, polychromatic and above all is *bhava pradhan* or emotionally sensitive. Objects in the Museum are torn away from their source and the Indian eye should restore them into their original home. This is the third eye of Indian art which sees objects in a museum with some concern. The Western eye delights in a museum. Does it have a third eye?

Purna, pratipurna and *sampurna* are different words for totality and wholeness that go beyond the limited psychological ideas of totality, to embrace the metaphysical concept of fullness or totality of being. *Purnatva* in its metaphysical essence means the coming together of two apparently opposite concepts or entities, like day and night, life and death. It is the richness of *purnatva* which accommodates opposites into a beautiful whole, and in doing so it demonstrates that, in it is in the merging or union of two dialectically opposite entities that *purnatva* arises, and it is in the understanding and realisation of that *purnatva* that we touch the highest reaches of the human condition. It is, as it were, standing on the earth that we reach for the stars. The Western mind, in preferring objective and rational reality, misses out in the beautiful idealised reality that is the hallmark of the Indian mind.

I was driving by a congested area of Mumbai and saw a potter making water pots. The potter is the archetypal artisan. He is an artist of the earth, who is involved in the many activities of working with the earth, who lives and functions in harmony with the world around him, the world of the trees and fruits, birds and blossoms, the waters and the wind, the sun and the sky, all of which are not just inert matter but deeply meaningful to him and have a living presence in his life and world view. The *kalasha* or the water pot is the primal and archetypical form; it arose from the churning of the ocean and contains *amrit* or nectar. It is this nectar that the gods drank and became immortal. The pot incorporates all the five cosmic elements in it: earth, water, fire, wind and space. The pot or the *kalasha* is the prototypical object of beauty for us. It obeys the principle of beauty beyond utility. Does the Grecian urn of English poetry have the same aesthetic and metaphysical beauty? I wonder.

भारतीय डाक
India Post

Kapila Vatsyayan, one of my mentors, once told me that there are two people who she considers enemies of Indian wisdom and they are Descartes and Freud. Descartes famously said, I think therefore I am, *ergo cogito sum,* suggesting that our very being depended on rational thought. Freud, on the other hand, posited the individual unconscious, which was the seat of our repressed sexual desires and fantasies, and it was this that was responsible for most of our psychological problems. The former posited that *buddhi* or the intellect is the farthest limit of the mind, and the latter posited the unconscious mind that is driven by sexual forces. We, in India, reject both of these propositions. We instead posit that the human mind is capable of going beyond the intellect into spheres like mysticism and that the mind is privy to the universal unconscious which is the seat of archetypal forms and behavior. In rejecting both Descartes and Freud, we in India celebrate a mind that is beautiful and goes far beyond the limitations of the ordinary Western mind. While rationality is the flag bearer of our intellect, there is a space above and beyond rationality, call it the super sensuous or mystical, which really defines us. We do not accept the individual unconscious of Freud but instead posit the universal unconscious, which stores shared archetypal forms for trackless generations and from which arise many of our cherished designs and forms. Move away Descartes and Freud. Let the Indian mind be as it is.

In this era of climate change and the voices that we hear from around the world it is well to remember the Indian view of nature. This world of nature is alive for us, the juice that enlivens it resonates with the sap that flows through us. Our own growth is tied to the fertility and fecundity of the world around us and even more, this world that we inhabit has not only a form but feeling as well. This is sometimes called a pagan worldview. The underlying Indian *drishti* or worldview is that of celebrating growth and fertility of the world of birds and blossoms, of venerating and worshipping the trees and the rivers, and worshipping the very earth upon which we stand and grow and let our mind and body resonate with the world of nature around us. The Prithvi Sukta of the Rg Veda composed almost 4000 years back, is a beautiful hymn and it is our homage to the earth. Only if the world would read it and follow it, we would not suffer from the ill effects of climate change that all of the Western world is talking about. We knew it 5000 years ago but sadly we in India have ignored it also.

It is fashionable these days to write books about understanding the world through hundred art objects. This is all very well and perhaps these books appeal to those who are urban westernised museum goers and who are satisfied with an art historical approach to Indian art. For them the collection of art objects represents the total wisdom of the world. However, the Indian eye demands to go beyond a superficial objective assessment of the art object. That eye does not regard the object as art, it prefers, the subjective to the objective and the idealised to the realistic, and looks for suggestions of the infinite and the eternal in the mute but beautiful object. The Indian eye is all about a *drishti* or insight that is synaesthetic, which sees with all the six senses, where all art forms come together, it feels even as it sees, and is interested in a serene inward experience of that object. This is our third eye. This subjective experience is restful and ultimately leads to a realisation of our own true selves. This is the ultimate purpose of engaging with the beautiful objects in a museum so that we can convert it into beauty. Shall we call this the Indian *drishti*, or the yoga of art with the third eye? Isn't it different from the Western eye, which revels in the experience of the museum and considers it the gold standard of aesthetic experience and imposes it on us even 75 years after we have gained independence?

लोदी रोड
प्रधान डाकघर
LODI ROAD
HEAD POST OFFICE
110003
भारतीय डाक
India Post

Western society is all about the individual, his freedom, his growth, his likes and dislikes, his friends and not so much about his family, his marriage, his work and eventually his old age spent in isolation in a retirement home! I suppose there are moments of glory and happiness in this individualistic and nuclear life style. By contrast for us in India, our life is all about the family and the community, our neighbours and neighbourhoods, our elders and even ancestors, our village. Surely we lose some of our privacy and individuality in this communal lifestyle, but we are never alone or isolated, never alienated from our fellow beings, there is no room for depression, even as we live in a multi-generational house, where the entire village is our home. The well known concept of *vasudhaiva kutumbakam*, the world is one family, starts from the village and spreads outwards. In the Western view your home is your castle where you preside largely unmindful of the world outside.

LETTERS

Fabrics in the Western world are mainly for clothes or furnishings. However in India, from times ancient, we have used fabrics to express some of our most cherished sentiments, whether it is to adorn or to decorate, to worship or to celebrate, to protect or to sanctify, to tell stories or to carry messages, as flags or as backdrops in our temples, as wall coverings in temples or home, as scrolls or wraps and also to clothe our bodies. Fabrics are central to the Indian world of art and adornment, rites and rituals, and also personal protection, privacy and dignity. A fragment of madder-dyed cotton has been found at Indus valley sites and it speaks initially of a highly sophisticated process of dyeing cotton 5000 years ago. Also, indigo vats have been discovered in artefacts of the Indus valley, and this attests to the presence of the dyeing technology of Indigo in times pre-historic. Fabrics were one of the earliest items that were traded and ancient Indian fabrics have been found in many parts of the world and India was known the world over in times ancient and also modern for its beautiful and colourful fabrics.

The Western view and concepts of fabrics is very limited.

The word border in the West conjures up something that divides and fragments. We in India create many borders, borders of saris and fabrics, of paintings and murals, frames or niches and in many different ways and for various reasons. Every border ultimately is the transition between the immediate and the ultimate, the microcosm and the macrocosm, the sacred and the secular, inside and outside, life and death, day and night, the finite and the infinite. And in creating and maintaining boundaries between apparently two bipolar opposites, the border in its own silent and eloquent way, suggests that while it is important to separate the two bipolar opposites, however ultimately the two are really one, two parts of a whole. There are no water tight compartments in nature, dawn moves into day and then into dusk. The boundary thus does not divide, but even while separating, it unites. The intention of the border is an invitation and exhortation of going forth from the confines of the border to that which is borderless, from the limited to infinity. The border initially divides, but ultimately unites. Can you think of a border like that in New York or in the Western modern mind?

Walk on Mumbai footpaths and you will see dirt and din, chaos and cacophony, poverty and penury, despair and degradation and much more. But look around, and you will see roadside shrines: a piece of stone coloured red placed under a tree, a photograph of a god placed on a tree and covered with flowers, a broken icon lovingly worshipped, a bell hung on a tree under which an unhewn stone is placed. What these shrines lack in sophistication they more than make up in being, unpretentious objects of veneration. You do not need officious priests but sincere faith and devotion. The plain folk who stand or rest there find peace and serenity. This is roadside spirituality, simple and sincere, and an essential part of the dispossessed and it rubs off on us even as we rush around in our luxury cars. Can you find this in the fancy sidewalks of New York?

2023/04/18 13:44

Western civilisation, both through church and state, is driven by a strong sense of ethical behavior. The Ten Commandments of Christianity, the fierce god of the Old Testament, the rules of Islam, are not only reinforced by the government but it imposes its own laws and bye-laws on society. The exact height of your cedar hedge, speed limits imposed on a deserted road in the middle of nowhere, insisting that you stand in line no matter, if by doing so you miss your flight, standing in line at a bank for almost an hour because the person before you was quibbling about an overcharge of five dollars, are some of the many examples of strictly enforced rules that come to mind. In India, we are also conscious of ethics, but when it comes to our wisdom texts and tradition, ethics is always contextual, and it is always presumed and not prescribed, and even more open to reinterpretation from one moment to the next depending on the circumstance.

Once Arvind Parikh, a friend and a renowned sitarist, asked his guru Vilayat Khan Sahib, "Why is that even though I play the sitar just as you taught me, I can never play it as well as you do?" Khan Sahib responded, "You can never be a great musician by sticking to the rules. You must get out of the strict rules of a raga, play in the free space, enjoy your freedom through your own creativity but then come back to the raga. This will increase your stature from a good musician to a great musician." This once again shows the shortcomings of rules and regulations in the achievement of greatness. Western music is written, Indian music is improvised. This is the fundamental difference between two cultures, not only in music but also in life. We say that there are rules, but rules should be broken, if they need to, if by doing so you are creating something beautiful.

We in India have been through invasions and colonisations, which have tried to subdue and even demolish us through the centuries. Despite that, our civilisation or *sanskriti* has been steadfast, imperishable, eternal. Therefore we call it *sanatana*, which is another word for the Hindu civilisation. It is not enough for us to say eternal, we must explain what the world eternal means. There are three main reasons for this. First, our civilisation is earth bound, we resonate with the rhythms of the earth, in that earth are our roots and in it we sow our seeds, it is with the seasons that our mind is coloured. Second, our *sanskriti* is not homocentric but multicentric. The world of nature, the trees and birds, the planets and the stars are a part of our universe and they with ours. Third, we are a joyous civilisation, *bhava pradhana* or emotionally driven and not one of guilt and sin. As long as the earth and the sky lives, so will our *sanskriti*. The white man of north America was able to ravage its native people. They could not do that to us because there is something eternal and indestructible about us like the stars and the seas.

Shringar or the romantic love between a man and as a woman is not only an exalted human emotion but the favorite of artists, both visual and performing. The Western mind is not able to keep romance pristine and pure, but very often connect it with lust and sex. One possible answer is that the Western tradition is anthropocentric and is not able to elevate romantic emotion beyond the realm of the humans. We in India are polycentric and we are able to see *shringar* in the world around us, in the world of trees and flowers, birds and bees and even move it to the heavens and connect it with our gods. When we see a creeper wind around the trunk of a tree, or two birds sitting on the same branch, when we see the earth and the sky come together when it rains, in all of this we see a romance, a coming together of *purusha* and *prakriti*, of spirit and matter. The genders, male and female for us are not sexually, but emotionally, defined and thus it is that romance for us is the transformation of sensuality of the two into the joyous spirituality of the one. The Western mind remains tied to Freud and his theories of repressed sexualities.

The Western tradition prides itself on the concept of perfection. Perfection for us can only apply to matters material. Objects can be perfect, a line can be perfectly straight, a mathematical problem can have a perfect solution, a machine can perform with perfect precision, an engineer or a carpenter can complete a job perfectly, activities can proceed with clock-like perfection. These are some of the many examples of perfection. We in India, favour *purnatva* or the state of totality rather than perfection. While we accept perfection as the end point of anything material, however a spiritual experience can only arise from a state of *purnatva*. In *purnatva*, while celebrating perfection, we also accept imperfection, in *purnatva* we bring two seemingly opposites together, in *purnatva* while living in finite spaces we always aspire for the infinite, in *purnatva* we favour continuous time and not linear time, in *purnatva* we go beyond the material and the psychologic to the ideal and the spiritual.

Indian thinking is contextual. The Indian word for this is *sandarbha* or *samyoga*. Nothing happens de novo, or by itself. A number of things have to come together for the successful completion of any activity. The planets have to be in concordance, the environment must be peaceful, our mind and body must be in harmony, and everyone we are involved with in synergy with us. *Samyoga* moves us from the Western homocentric universe to a multicentric Indian world, where man is not alone but in a web of interconnections. The Indian view of life limits the individual and upholds the collective. The Western view leads to loneliness and alienation, as they stand alone. The Indian view is one of community and therefore of belonging, it fosters relationships, builds bridges, holds hands, embraces, stoops to pick up anyone that has fallen and also will fold its hands to venerate anyone higher than them. Context widens the moment and the individual to something much larger.

Closely related to *sandarbha* is the concept of *mangalya* or auspiciousness, which the Western mind fails to understand deeply. *Mangalya* implies ideas like wholesome, beneficial, noble, leading to prosperity and well being. *Mangal* is not so much for the individual but for the entire community. The goddess of *mangalya* is Lakshmi who arises from the primal myth of churning of the ocean. Lakshmi is both a goddess and a secular symbol. In the Western mind, driven as it is by rationality, there is little or no room for what is *mangal* which is both sacred and secular, rational and mystical at the same time, as initially the two are dichotomous. The Indian mind is able to hold the two opposites together which the Western mind cannot. This is an asset and leads to a richer, robust Indian mind. *Mangalya* is a multi-nuanced concept and is expressed in word, costume, gesture, colour, lyrics, image and space.

JEWELLERS
भारतीय डाक
India Post
चम्बा
प्रधान डाकघर
CHAMBA
HEAD POST OFFICE, CHAMBA (H.P.)

The word myth in day-to-day parlance in English means something that is not real or fictitious, not worthy of serious attention, and which is not the truth and therefore best given up. However mythic stories, called *gathas* and *kathas*, are an alternative source of knowledge for us. These mythic narratives form the bedrock of secterian Hinduism or *sampradays*, it is the source of our gods and goddesses, our icons in temples and shrines, nay our entire religious edifice rests on these myths. Myth for us is real, both aesthetically and religiously, and the onus is on us to assert its reality. On its surface mythic narratives are full of poetic imagination and not historic reality, but they are beautiful and it behooves us to mythify our life, in other words make myths a part of our daily life and living, either aesthetically or religiously. Although the modern Western mind has privy to Greek myths, myths in general have no part of their mind. Today's Western world has forgotten its ancient myths.

When I once asked a prominent Indian artist why he painted the way he did, he asked me, "Do you ever see a straight line in nature?" He was so right. In the world of nature we have lines that turn and twist, sing and dance, spiral up and down, curve and wind, and thus they create the beautiful and varied forms that we so admire: the leaves and the flowers, the birds and the bees, the river and the cloud. The Indian mind delights in the curved and the wavy line, it represents its emotionality, its life, its ability to bend with the wind and rise to the sky, for it is a *bhava pradhana*, view of life. Our *rachana* or designs, our *sangeet* or music, our painting and architecture, celebrate the wavy and dancing line. A straight line suggests rationality and an arid intellectual or *buddhi pradhana* view of life of the Western mind. The wavy, curvaceous, singing line is the signature of Indian arts and crafts which enriches our life, and is one of the many ways in which the Indian tradition is different from that of the West. Long live the difference!

The watchword of the Indian civilisation is pluralism. Multilayered are our religious beliefs, manifold are our customs, many are our languages, varied our cuisine, multicoloured our costumes, various our sounds and rhythms and numerous our fairs and festivals. When one travels the length and breadth of the country, the landscape changes and so do our languages, we see Hindu temples and Muslim mosques, Jainas and Buddhists celebraing their faith, and Parsis and Christians reading their holy books. Despite religious and social discord that one sees lately, there is an underlying and abiding unity and harmony which the foreign eye fails to see and experience. There is an invisible, thread that ties us together, which fosters unity in diversity, celebrates our pluralistic traditions, it is neither monolithic nor monochromatic, it accepts dichotomies and does not force unitarianism and proudly says: *ekam sat, bahudha vipra vadanti*, Truth is one, the wise call it by different names. Can the Western world view do this? Their multiculturalism is of the melting pot variety where you give up your identity and dissolve yourself into one homogenous whole. Homogeneity is not a part of the Hindu ethos, where while remaining tied to each other in the web of life, we maintain our own identity.

Aadhaar ATM
India Post
NO PARKING
PINCODE OF THIS AREA IS
400 035
RAJ BHAVAN
400 035
Rubber tree
Ficus elastica Roxb.

We all want law and order in our lives, we feel secure when it is enforced, and in its absence we feel threatened. We reject chaos as a lower order of being, a state of being uncivilized, uncultured. This however is largely a Western state of the human mind which is driven by arid rationality and limited logical thinking. In India, we accept chaos as a primal state of being, an essential first step in our evolution, a state of the human condition which we must accept as the starting point of our civilization and the world around us. We embrace chaos and disorder, and accept that the move to order from chaos is a seamless transformation. Chaos and order are not two dichotomous states for us in India but a movement from one to another. This movement from chaos to order is akin to yoga. This primal chaos reminds us of the myth of the churning of the ocean from which emerge the nine treasures for us. Recognising chaos and disorder as a starting point in our contemplation urges us to move forward and upward from it to more serene and peaceful states of mind.

One of many concepts that divides the Indian and the Western world view is the concept of time. We see this very clearly in paintings. Paintings from the Mughal atelier very often show a courtly scene frozen in time. There is no movement, but just a moment. Rich in detail and robust in its depiction of the court and its paraphernalia, Mughal paintings are inspired by Western academic realism which celebrates moments rather than movement. Rajput paintings on the other hand shows movement, a continuity without fragmentation, linear time that morphs into continuous or circular time. Taking Krishna paintings as an example, the Rajput artist will show multiple Krishnas moving across the canvas, and as we follow Him, the small space of the miniature painting creates a narrative. Fractured time of Western and Mughal painting is a fault line, that eventually leads to multiple fractures in our psyche. Continuous time which defines the Indian psyche on the other hand provides stability, an unbroken *akhanda* state of mind.

If I were asked to thank someone from the past it would have to be the Vedic poets. 5000 years ago, they were the custodians of the truth and they spoke about it in beautiful words or poetry. There were no commandments, no rules, nothing was forbidden; instead we are asked to experience beauty through their words. Poetic truth came much before religious or metaphysical truth for us in India and poetry remains the benchmark for anything beautiful. All our art bears a poetic stamp, it moves from the sensual to the spiritual and from secular to the sacred without any fragmentation. Our Vedic poets were called *rishis* or seers, also *prajapatis* or leaders of the community. They gave us a vision of ultimate reality through their mellifluous words. There were no idols, no temples. no gods as we commonly understand. Their poetry arose from their radiant imagination or *pratibha*. To those Vedic poets, my *shat shat pranams*, hundred upon hundred salutations. If that question were to be put to a Westerner what would they say? Socrates, Plato, Aristotle, or perhaps their forefathers. Did they enunciate poetic truth as we did?

Most of us use the phrase "rooted" when we refer to feeling settled in a place or community. We feel a sense of belonging, have made friends, understood the system and feel comfortable with the rhythms of daily life. This is true in Mumbai as it is in New York. However there is a big difference in the way in which we understand "rooted" in India. There is an image of a tree in the Rg Veda and also in the Gita. This is called an "upside down tree" with its roots in the sky and branches spreading below. This is a very evocative image. Our roots are in things celestial or spiritual. Being rooted sociologically and psychologically is important in our quotidian life, but more important it is for us to be rooted in our enduring religious and spiritual values. If we succeed in doing this we will be secure materially and spiritually. Perhaps we should be rooted both in the earth and the sky.

In the modern West Nature, or the world around us, was for exploitation for our own needs and wants, our desires and consumption. Fortunately in the last few decades the ecology movement has caught on and there is greater awareness of protecting our environment. Climate change and the fear of our planet disintegrating is very real. In ancient India we respected our environment, whether it were our trees or rivers, our land and our birds and animals. It will not be an exaggeration to say that Indic consciousness is never far from trees, forests, animals and birds. Unlike the human centered cultures of the West, where the entire Nature is seen as a platter served up for human consumption, Indic culture teaches us to worship life in its varied forms. It underlines a oneness of life in all creation, where your relationships with your inner self, with society and with Nature are not different silos but integrated as an organic whole. Drive along any road in Mumbai and you will see trees being worshipped. Most of our art has the imprint of nature in it. Indian design celebrates the shapes and textures of Nature. It is this that takes away from the Western homocentric world to our world where we say with Tukaram, a 16th century singer saint from Maharashtra, *vriksha valli amare soyare*, the trees and the creepers are our family. The Indian ecology movement started centuries back.

You have heard of the Procrustean bed, I am sure. Procrustes was an innkeeper and would offer the bed to visitors. However, if the visitor was too tall for the bed he would cut off his legs and if the visitor was too short he would stretch him out till he fitted the bed. And then there is Hobson's Choice: you had a choice of renting a horse, the first horse on the left, which happened to be lame, or none at all. To me both these apocryphal stories suggest that the hospitality they offered was only to suit them but not the visitor. I call this contrived or measured hospitality. We, on the other hand, in India, say *atithi devo bhava*, a visitor is like god. Even the word *atithi* means one who comes without an appointment. We in India will open our door to anyone who knocks and share whatever food we have. Our hospitality is warm and genuine. You see this in rural India more than in the cities. City dwellers have become jaded and suspicious of anyone unknown knocking on their door, but Indian hospitality is real and richer. Even more we in India will not let our visitor leave without sharing food or water.

भारतीय डाक
India Post
पत्र
India Post

Emigration of Indian people has been going on for centuries and Indian settlements are well known in East and West Indies, Europe and now North America. My concern is with Hinduism in the diaspora: what is its tenor and texture and is it different from that of its origins in India? The answer from me, is of course yes. Hinduism in the diaspora is semitised, schizophrenic and santised and is one step removed from Hinduism in India. There are many answers to this conundrum, but one that appeals to me the most is to look at the pristine times when Hinduism, not by that name, came to be formulated in India, also not by that name, as both India and Hindu are foreign terms. The Vedic *rishis*, if we accept that as the starting point of Hinduism, were wonderstruck by the lush tropical country, with its fertility and fecundity of trees and blossoms, clear blue skies with the sun, the moon and the planets, and sparkling waters. It is this geography that led to the development of fundamental Hindu ideas of pluralism and multiple approaches to truth, and not just a monolithic and absolute truth of desert born religions. The absence of a prophet or a messiah led to the Hindu penchant of self-exploration, into inward thinking and even more, going beyond rational thought to mystical thought. Hindu ideas as they developed from the Vedas onwards took into account social realities of the day, sociologic and political, and exposure to those social realities is as important to the experience of Hindu wisdom as is the inward search. If you want to be a true Hindu ,you have to be in the geographic India. If you are satisfied being a diaspora Hindu, you can live in Timbaktu.

What is the semitised, schizophrenic and sanitized Hinduism in the diaspora, you may ask. Let me tell you. We in India accept chaos and confusion, dirt and disorder, as a part of our life. In saying that I am not saying that we like these situations, but we negotiate our way around it, accepting it as a part of the human condition. Order and disorder are not two dichotomous opposites but a continuum. Temples in the diaspora are neat and clean, orderly and organised; this is what I call sanitised. The Western world to the Hindu mind is schizophrenic because it considers the sacred and the secular as dichotomous, while for us it is, once again, a continuum. And lastly visits to a temple look more and more like the Sunday morning service at a church, where you show up on a Sunday morning, take part in a communal worship and then have a meal. To the traditional Hindu mind this is jarring. Even more, we come to expect that life should be orderly and free of chaos and confusion and when it is not we are uncomfortable, and wish it were not so. To find order in the midst of disorder, peace in the midst of confusion, and beauty even when surrounded by what is ugly, is the mark of a Hindu mind. Can an average Westerner accept this?

When an individual or society, as in the modern Western world, is driven by ethics there is the danger that ethics becomes the end all and be all of life. An ethical view of life would be to say, "Once I have discharged myself ethically I need not do anything more. Why run the extra mile when I have followed all the ethical norms? Why should I be compassionate when I have been ethical? I am a law abiding citizen, paying my taxes and breaking no rules: need I do anything more? Yes. For us in the Indian tradition ethics is just the starting point of a noble person. *Samvedana* or a compassionate heart, care and concern not just for the person but for his entire family, a charitable disposition, correcting social evils, giving a helping hand to anyone in need, lifting the downtrodden, all of this goes beyond ethics. Ethics for us is important, but not sufficient by itself.

The Western mind is driven by intellect and rationality, it is what we call *bhava pradhan*. The Indian mind on the other hand is driven by emotion and mysticism, it is *bhava pradhan* and *gudha pradhan*, emotional and mystical. We do not negate *buddhi*, we do not discard rationality, but we are keenly aware that our mind has other realms, many other layers, above and beyond the intellect, that our mind is not a square box but a *mandala*. A *mandala* is where there are many entrances to its space and in that space we let various forces interact and bring them to a point of stillness or the *bindu*. We accept emotion as an integral part of life and the human condition. Even more, we luxuriate in mystical thoughts, indulge in dream like states, accept abstract states of being, assert that rationality is not the only metric of life. We readily turn to astrology, talk to psychics, turn to godmen, while standing firm on the earth we raise our hands in wonder at the sky, make images of our gods but then lovingly deposit them in the river, we worship many forms of the divine but then accept the formless as the ultimate. We live in linear time but at the back of our mind is the concept of continuous and circular time and even more of a state of timelessness. There are vistas above seeing and understanding the world rationally. The modern Western mind abides in rationality.

A common phrase that is heard commonly in our everyday Western world is R&R, or rest and relaxation. "I am resting as I am on my break, I am tired and I need a holiday, I desperately need to go away for a R&R." There is nothing wrong with these expressions, very natural when you are in the work force or in the rat race for the American dream. But have you wondered about the many different meanings of rest or *vishranti* for us in India? For the committed person, rest is only a short interruption of work, so that he can continue working even harder. What about metaphysical rest? That rest is to realise that at the centre of movement is stillness, that in the midst of the cacophony of sounds one should feel silence, that in the progression of life or *pravritti* one should think of *nivritti* or cessation, that all forms must ultimately rest in the formless. This is the essence of Vedanta. And finally there is what I call aesthetic rest, where after indulging and experiencing what is beautiful one then retreats into our inner mind and rests in the beauty and serenity of that mind. The next time you think of rest you should perhaps think also of the many different kinds of rest for us in India.

For us in India, especially in the Hindu tradition, everything has a meaning, not just a purpose. Nothing is out of place, no occurrence is accidental, no relationship is casual, an object is not just an object, no life is without a purpose, every thought and feeling has a reason. In other words, in what appears on the surface as chaotic or disorderly, there is a deeper purpose, a hidden metaphor and a meaning. This meaning may not be apparent on first sight, just as a metaphor needs decoding, the event or relationship which may be totally unconnected to the superficial view of your life may a deeper meaning, when you are faced with a problem you might even wonder whether there is any justice in this world. However, under the surface everything is connected, what appears meaningless on the surface has a meaning on careful contemplation. When you do not find a meaning perhaps you are not going under the surface. In attributing a meaning to everything we are recognizing that there is a certain cosmic order, *rta* in Vedic terms, that is much greater than our small strength to control our lives. In Western society, everything has a purpose, a utility, a transaction, but not meaning, and when the purpose or transaction is over it is time to discard it and walk away from it. The Western civilisaiton believes that mankind can control their own destiny. Nothing is accidental for us in the Indian wisdom traditions. Everything has a meaning, an *artha*, a cosmic order.

The other day, a friend though he is a Christian, who is better versed in Hindu thought than many Hindus, said to me, "In the 21st century we will have to redefine god". This caught my ear and the sentence resonated with me for days. Who was the "we" that he was talking about? Christians? Jews? Muslims? Certainly not Hindus, I said to myself. For we Hindus have no gods, therefore where is the problem of redefining them? The question or defining god is essentially a Abrahamic situation. Their god is God, an absolute being, sometimes merciful, at other times revengeful, sometimes forgiving and at other times punishing. Can this kind of God stand up in the 21st century, with science and technology controlling our life, a life that is shaped mainly by ethics and aesthetics and not metaphysics? People in the Western world have more faith in technology than in the church, and anything that it can offer, other than solace. But solace is not knowledge, it is not *brahmajnana* or transcendent knowledge. *Brahmajnana* is a state of peace and serenity, awareness and realisation. As Tagore said, *anandaloke mangalaloke satya sundaro birajo*, Truth and beauty for us reside in the realm of *ananda* and the auspicious. This *brahmajnana* resides in us, and not in any far away place in the heavens. *Brahmajnana* is untouched by the social realities of the day, it is eternal and constant. It never has to be defined, only felt. Where is the question of redefining it?

When someone asked me the other day why I went to India so often and for so long, I immediately answered, "Because my search for my gods is easier in India than here in Canada." This of course led to the second question, "Who are your gods?" I welcomed both those questions, as it gave me an opportunity to not only examine my own position regarding the sacred and the divine, but express it cogently to others. Please note that I spell god with a small g, signalling that I do not subscribe to the Abrahamic absolute God, with a capital G. For me Truth is god and not the other way around and that Truth for me is in the experience of things beautiful. I get those experiences of the beautiful in so many places in Mumbai: driving by roadside shrines, casual conversations with people on the street which invariably has some reference to the divine, going to music concerts and dance performances, teaching and sharing with students whatever I have learnt, sitting under a tree and watching the world go by, spending time sitting in galleries of a museum, wandering in and out of antique shops, strolling in the Robber's Market, having a cup of tea and bun *maska* in a Irani restaurant, discussing the fine points of a 16th century Krishna painting or reading an ancient manuscript with a scholar and so many more things that I can do in Mumbai, that I cannot do in Ottawa. You might ask, do I really find my gods there or is it only a "time pass" as they say in Mumbai? Yes, I do find my gods there. I will answer that in the next postcard.

I find my gods when *satya* or truth and *saundarya* or beauty come together. In other words, it is in aesthetic experiences, more than any other, that I find my gods in Mumbai. The core of aesthetic experience is *ananda*, or an inward, serene state of bliss, above the dichotomies of *samsara* that results from engagement with a beautiful object. Those aesthetic experiences can come from classical art objects as in a museum or art gallery, but they can equally come from everyday objects that are beautifully made, such as a brass *lota* or a piece of embroidery. I derive aesthetic experiences from language and literature, gesture and ritual, which are everywhere in Mumbai. On the fringes of aesthetic experiences for me in Mumbai, are experiences of *karuna* or compassion or *bhakti* or surrender, that I encounter in streets and shops, museums and markets, reminding me that aesthetic experiences are not only from the gods of India. It is to my gods of beauty that I want to return again and again, and it is that which gives meaning, direction and purpose to my life. Try it. It might work for you as well.

Staying with art and aesthetic experiences I have, once again, a dissenting view from that of the modern West. In the West, individuality is paramount and when it comes to art, the artist is as important as the art object. Thus we speak of this is a Picasso, or this is a Monet and so on. When we bring in the artist into one's aesthetic experience, you are willynilly opening the door to a personality cult of the artist and everything sociologic. What if I do not like Picasso as a human being, will this not interfere with my experience of his art? In ancient and medieval India, art was generally, though not totally, anonymous. Even more, the various *akritis* or forms, the motifs and metaphors, belong to the community and not to the individual. These artistic devices are archetypal and stored in the universal subconscious and are a treasure of the community, and passed down through trackless generations. Art, therefore for us, is a collective experience, whereas in the West, it is largely an individual experience, the only exception being music and ballet. I am afraid this has crept into contemporary India as well, so that we have a Hussain horse and a Raza *bindu*. I prefer to keep the art object separate from the artist and derive a pure aesthetic experience without art history. This is more robust and richer.

In the vast treasure of Indian paintings it is Mughal painting that comes closest to modern painting from the West, and that is why Western trained Indian art historians feel that Mughal paintings are the gold standard of Indian painting. Mughal paintings, with their emphasis on rational depiction of a historical moment, (eg. Akbarnama) along with the three point vanishing perspective, is true to the rational outlook of the Western mind. We in India, prefer the narrative style of painting, where we generally show three moments, the present, the past and the future all in one frame. Indian paintings while not adopting the three point rational perspective, generally show the sky, thereby introducing the concept of the sacred and the divine. This fits in not only with our sense of continuous, circular and eternal time but that the sacred and the secular are a continuum. While Western thought favours fragmentation and separation of the sacred and the secular, Indian thought delights in its continuity. We in India never forget the sky, both real and metaphoric, for it is the home of the formless ultimate.

A *mandapa*, and there are many *mandapas*, is a special enclosure for a variety of activities for us. We have *ranga mandapas*, a pavilion in a temple, a *lagna mandapa*, for marriage, *pranay mandapa*, a space in a *haveli* for amorous pleasures, *sabha mandapa*, a space for public activities, *nritya mandapa*, a proscenium for theatre. Our first mythic *mandapa* was one that was built by Vishvakarma, the divine architect, for the performance of our first dance performance as stipulated by Bharata in the Natyashastra, 1st century BCE. In essence, a *mandapa* has a floor, a ceiling and pillars. The floor is our earth, the ceiling the sky and the pillars are the Indra *stambha*, the first pillar that separated the earth and the sky. Various demigods were placed in all the eight directions of the *mandapa*. Thus the *mandapa* was a recreation of the cosmic space here on earth and assured a certain sanctity and sacrality to it and to the event that was taking place in it. This is one of many examples of how we create spaces which combine beauty and sacredness. Is there an example that you can give me from such spaces in the West? The salon of the West does not capture for me the cosmic resonance of the *mandapa*.

Immanuel Kant (1724-1804), the German philosopher, wrote his famous answer to the question set by a Berlin journal: 'What is Enlightenment?' He began by quoting the Latin poet Horace (20 BCE), 'Sapere aude, dare to know'. Kant felt that mankind needs to emerge from its self-imposed immaturity to use one's own reason and without guidance from someone else. Have the courage, Kant says, to use your own intellect and this is therefore a motto of the Enlightenment. There are two features of this that goes counter to the Indian view of knowledge. Knowledge is not only intellectual and for us is ever present, innate and eternal. We as humans, have forgotten it and we need to discover it through contemplation and not create it with reason and intellect. Also, for us a guru, or a spiritual teacher, is indispensable. If Kant is the spokesperson of the modern Western tradition, it is Vedanta that speaks for us, and the two are not the same.

Let me tell you about a fundamental Hindu idea, with some examples: after Ganesha is lovingly worshipped for 10 days, He is then deposited in the sea or river. A scroll that is torn and frayed is placed in the river and a new one made. A lamp that is lit and floated in the river disintegrates in its waters. *Nirmalya* or left over flowers from worship are offered to a river .A votive horse is placed under a tree where it disintegrates over time and a new horse is made by the *adivasi* from the same earth the next year. A *rangoli* from the previous day is wiped out and a new *rangoli* is made everyday. All of these are examples of a fundamental Hindu idea that the form cannot remain static, and to fulfil itself must become formless, all metaphysical concepts are important but must eventually be given up to emptiness, all sacred words must in the end become silent, and every movement must dissolve in stillness. Ultimate reality for us is *nirakar* or formless. However, the journey from form to formless has to be negotiated lovingly and not with trauma. Only then will the formless be born into a new and beautiful form. The average Western mind would find it hard to deconstruct what it has constructed in the realm of metaphysics. More about this in my next postcard.

प्रवेश
ENTRY
डाक भवन
DAK BHAWAN
C-12
पैकेट
PACKETS
पत्र
LETTERS
C-11
110001
पैकेट
PACKETS

To deconstruct what one has constructed is the hallmark of what is called Idealist or mystical Hindu and Buddhist thinking. Nothing that the human hand or mind constructs is totally permanent, nor is it meant to be. What is very unusual here, and different from most other religions, is that even god, or the images that we worship, are also impermanent, they too are but stepping stones. Not many religions put the responsibility on the adherent to put his gods aside as well, on the journey to ultimate reality. The question then is what is permanent, eternal, unchanging, undecaying, timeless or *sanatana* for the human condition? In its most basic sense creation is timeless and cyclical, going from activity to rest and back to activity again and at the root of this cycle of creation, is creativity or *sarjanatmakta*. Creation arises when Purusha and Prakriti, Spirit and Matter, Male and Female interact, which makes *shringar* or love as the basis of all creation. So it is with love that we must let go of the form into the formless and it is with love that we need to come back into this world with a new form. A common line that is heard in Canada is, 'What goes around comes around.' Do they mean it in the Indian sense. I doubt it.

The other day I came across a statement by a German philosopher, who, when he was asked, "What is life?" answered, "Life is the longing to manifest." To manifest is to grow, to flourish, to prosper, to expand. That fits in with my view and assessment of the West and the American motto, 'Life, Liberty and the Pursuit of Happiness.' As an Indian, if I were asked the same question, I would answer, "Life is the opportunity to know yourself, to the Vedantic *mahavakya*, to realise *aham brahmasmi*." The Western view is to grow outwards, the Indian view is to search inwards. The inward search in the Indian view, is not to ignore the outer material world, but to start outwards but then turn inwards, for that is where your real self is. That turning inwards means opening the third eye. More about the third eye in my next postcard.

The eyes, it is said, are the most expressive part of the body, they are a mirror of the mind and a window of our *atman*. Poets speak of the fisheyed Minakshi, the consort of Shiva, the doe eyed Bani Thani of Kishangarh, the dancing eyes of the *nayika* of Bhartrhari and the arrow like eyes of Amaru's *nayikas*, the teasing eyes of the dancer, the alluring eyes of the *surasundari*, the beautiful woman, and the inviting eyes of the *apsara*. To see is to know, when the eyes are open or *unmesh*, we understand the world around us, when the eyes are closed or *nimesh* we contemplate, when eyes flutter they are marking time, when they cry they express sadness but the best of all, when the eyes are joyous they speak of the beauty of what we behold whether it is the bountiful nature around us or the smile of our beloved but when eyes of the lover and the beloved meet it is an assurance that their love is sacred. The third eye is the contemplative eye, the eye that brings the art object to life, it is the eye that creates *purnatva* or fullness to aesthetic experience, it is the eye of insight, of our *drishti*. To be continued.

For that third eye is synaesthetic and polychromatic, it is that eye that lets you taste the various *rasas* and decode the many metaphors in our art, it is that eye that while letting us stand on earth takes us beyond space and time through our art objects, it is that eye that ensures that the various myths that we represent in our art are a reality and not *mythia* or false, it is that eye that takes us beyond the comfort of rational thought to that secret and mystical spaces in our mind where we are closest to the truth of our own being, it is that eye that responds and finds stillness in movement, it is that eye that finds the *akar* or abstract form of the *akriti* or beautiful form and the *rekha* or line of the *rachana* or composition. I began by saying that I do not want to speak about the third eye of Shiva, but yet I was wrong. The third eye of Shiva is indeed the eye of wrath but it is that eye of Shiva that urges us to move from *avidya* to *vidya,* from ignorance to knowledge and using that metaphor we can think of the third eye of Indian art. Dear Western art lovers, do you have a third eye?

The rational view of the world, for that is the signature of the modern, enlightened, West, is afraid of contradictions, afraid that a rational mind cannot hold the two in the same space, to do so would be to disturb the man made order in this world, to accept order and deny disorder, to degrade rationality and accept a lower order of thinking. But that is exactly where the Indic view triumphs. We in Hindu/India believe that reality is made up of two opposite truths: day and night, life and death, male and female, rational and emotional, longing and belonging, *dvaita* and *advaita*, duality and non-duality, *bhakti* and *jnana,* devotion and knowledgde. The Shri Yantra of two opposing triangles, intersecting each other and creating a space where the lotus blooms, is one of the best examples of the Hindu mind which gladly accepts two opposite realities and brings it together in a organic holistic whole. In that way we are not denying the contradictions, but rising above them and creating a new higher reality. One of the most beautiful icons of this is the Ardhanarisvara, the half Shiva, half Parvati. I do not think the modern West has anything similar and so profoundly insightful.

Tagore writes, "There is a point where in the mystery of existence contradictions meet, where movement is not at all movement and stillness is not at all stillness, where the idea and the form, the within and without are united; where infinite becomes finite, yet not losing its infinity. If this meaning is dissolved then things become unreal." We in Indic thought, prefer to leave the ultimate answer to existential questions as an unsolvable mystery, and not a difficult to solve problem. The latter is the way of the West, the former the way of Indian wisdom. For us, mystery is not a problem, it is a very beautiful space in our mind, where the finite reaches out to the infinite, the temporal to the timeless, the bounded to the free, the spoken to the silent and the human stands in front of the divine in reverence. In that moment all questions are silenced, all doubts resolved in a beautiful effulgence of wonder and thus the mind is led to larger and more beautiful vistas.

Cut flowers in a vase is a common artistic motif in Western paintings as it is in home adornments. This goes counter to the traditional Indian view of life and aesthetic practice. Cutting flowers not only causes trauma to the plant, but to enjoy them in a painting or in the home is to suggest fragmentation and division, rather than continuity and an organic whole. The Indian penchant is to use the meandering lotus vine as artistic adornment. Though this vine is not a botanical reality it emphasises continuity, an unbroken state, *purnatva*. In the same vein, are traditional fabrics worn by women and men. Traditionally we in India do not wear stitched fabrics which involves using a needle as well cutting. Thus *sari*, *odhni*, *angavastra*, *dhoti* and *pheta* are the traditional fabrics. The emphasis is to point to higher reality being continuous and not broken or fragmented, not intellectually understood but intuitively and mystically realised.

The Jaina wisdom texts speak of *anekantavada*, which says that answers to questions of higher reality should be answered with a "yes" and "no" at the same. Thus to the question, "Does God exist"?, the answer is "yes and no," While a rational answer to that question would be either yes or no, in answering a question with two opposites one is positing a reality that is above and beyond rational constructs. So does this attitude apply only to questions of higher reality? Yes it does. Once we accept that dictum, many ordinary questions can also be answered with a yes and no. To the question, "Will I succeed in what I am doing?" one should also answer yes and no, suggesting that while we should strive for success, it is by no means guaranteed, and that we should accept the outcome with equanimity. This is the message of the oft repeated message from the Gita as well. The modern West is driven by a single pointed rationality which does not admit contradictions.

A friend who owns a car dealership related to me an episode. He was expanding the facilities of his Service department and was adding two more service bays. This required that the land be dug and cement be poured into it. Before that happened he went there, asked that the work be stopped, placed a coconut, a two dollar coin and a betel nut (*supari*) into the space and joined his hands in prayer. The workers did not know why he did that and they asked him to explain. He said that any construction meant violence to the earth, and since the earth was sacred to the Hindus, he offered a little prayer asking for its forgiveness. His Western counterpart would have a land breaking ceremony but would it have the same significance? Many Hindus when they get out of the home in morning offer salutations to the earth before stepping on it. A dancer, a musician or a singer would in the same sentiment touch the stage, which is a representation of the earth, with veneration before stepping on it. Don't you think that our view of the earth is very different from that of the modern West? When you have some time read the Pritivi Sukta, Hymn to the Earth, in the Vedas.

These days there is a lot of talk of inflation and the rising cost of living both in Canada and the U.S.A. The so called Consumer Price Index or CPI is based on what is called a basket of goods. But what if I do not consume many of the items that are in the basket like meat and alcohol? The CPI does not apply to me. Sombre faced Politicians and Economists are screaming about various remedies that should be brought in. Political observers are blaming this party and the other. On our kitchen table, while we feel deeply about those who suffer because of rising costs, quite a different Economist is speaking to us. He tells us much of our problem is that our wants are greater than our needs and if we only made that equation more equitable, life would be a lot simpler, for after all he says, that there is more to life than increasing its speed. That Economist for us is Mahatma Gandhi, who sadly matters very little to many who read these postcards. Incidentally my idea of writing postcards comes from him. The Capitalist Economy of the Western world, based on borrow and spend, is very alluring, but at the end of the day, it is a trap. Frugality, sharing and saving for a rainy day are watchwords for those of us from India.

It is widely known that while many mathematicians across the world were engaged in creating the mathematical zero or *shunya*, it was Aryabhatta in the 5th century CE in India who gave it a formal basis. What is even more interesting that this concept of *shunya* or zero is very similar to the Buddhist concept of *shunyata* or emptiness. Which proves once again, that major ideas can only emerge when there is an underlying bedrock or ethos out of which it grows. The political concept of *Ahimsa* or non-violence of Gandhi can only have emerged from the Jaina ethos of India. The concept of Radha by Jayadeva can only emerge in eastern India where Tantra was mainstream. Hinduism as a religion and a system of thought can only emerge from the geographical ancient India. Socio-historic environment and metaphysical wisdom are tied. That is why I feel that Hindu thought thrives and is best understood and experienced best in the geographical India.

The concept of *shunya* as void was a source of great anxiety to the ancient Greeks and also to the early Hindus. It was not until the second generation or Mahayana Buddhists came along and postulated the concept of *shunayta* or emptiness, that both Hindus and Buddhists alike accepted, that emptiness can be robust and rich, it represents a mind devoid of the clutter of concepts and beliefs, of fear and superstition, where there are no binaries, a still mind like a lake of clear water where there are no weeds and where the sun shines, where our entire being rests like a *bindu* or seed capable of growing into a tree. The modern Western mind driven as it by *pravritti* or progress and growth, finds it difficult to accept the beauty and richness of *shunyata*, that rest is as important as activity, and it is only during the experience of *shunayta* that we really know ourselves. I have heard the phrase, still waters run deep. Would the modern Western mind accept it metaphysically or just psychologically?

In an era of globilisation, India's intellectual properties are also being exported for widespread consumption. Ideas like yoga, *ahimsa*, meditation, mindfulness, among others. All of these ideas lose their pristine meaning and are taken out of context and are transformed into something lesser than what they were. Yoga becomes a form of exercise, *ahimsa* becomes a political slogan for peace, meditation is for relaxation and reducing stress, mindfulness is an activity when you have nothing to do! Where is Patanjali, Mahavira and Buddha in all of these? I have no problem in today's Western person using Indian ideas in whatever way they want. At least they are not using them for any anti-social acitivities. But it does remind us of a fundamental truth that I have always believed in, and that is, Hindu, Buddhist and Jaina ideas arose in the geographical India, and they are best understood in that land. Yoga in traditional India is not the same as yoga in New York.

The Western tradition, driven as it is by science and rationality, insists on finding the causes of things, not just the immediate cause but the primal cause, say of creation or even beauty. The motto of the Royal Institute of Science in Bombay was, "It is good to find out the causes of things." But can we always do that, and even if we did, will it satisfy us deeply? Perhaps it would give us psychological comfort in finding the cause. Instead, the Indic wisdom is that the origins of many profound and beautiful things, and also of everyday emotions like love, should be left as a beautiful mystery to be enjoyed and not a problem to be solved. Trying to solve the problem and find the cause would be like plucking the petals of a flower to see where the aroma was coming from! Can we also leave god in the same beautiful mystery rather than attempting to define it rationally?

There are many differences, among others, between the present day India and the current modern West. In today's India modernity is not uniform and is mixed with the pre-modern, it is an admixture of the rural and the urban, the rational intellectual and the ancient pagan. Indian modern artists did not fit the trope of 'modernists' in the Western definition of modernism, as they were living out the actual transition from colonialism to nationalism. One example comes to mind. When the Indian Space Research Organisation launched its first satellite, the scientists at ISRO first performed a *puja,* a ritual worship and prayer, to invoke the blessings of the gods. When we buy a car we break a coconut and hang a garland on it as we bring it home. We worship the earth even as we build a sky scraper on it. When new tennis courts were commissioned at the Willingdon Club in Mumbai the markers and the ball boys performed a simple religious ceremony. The Indian psyche can never be totally modern as we like to return to our ancient and the past even as we straddle the modern and the rational. Our psyche can contain both, without any contradictions. The modern West has forgotten, even denying its roots, and in so doing is denying some of the richness of the pre-modern traditions.

Ours is an ancient civilisation and our mind is coloured by images of trees, forests, animals and birds, as also rivers and pastoral spaces all of which become archetypes. Our psyche is agricultural and for us the potter is not only the first maker of objects but is also a philosopher of the earth. One commonly hear phrases like, “I love Nature” or “I love the outdoors”. Beyond a certain point, these and similar statements, do not mean very much. All they are saying is that they are happy and they feel relaxed to be with Nature and outdoors. But there is more to Nature for us than getting a sense of relaxation or comfort, it should be a source of knowledge or *atmabodh*. Indic culture teaches us to worship life in its varied natural forms. It underlines a oneness of life in all creation, where your relationship with your inner self, with society and with Nature are not different silos but integrated as an organic whole. Nature teaches us the cyclical nature of growth, decay and regeneration, of how a seed grows into a tree which then grows to touch the sky. The tree, as it grows from the netherworld towards the heavens, becomes the axis mundi or the Indra *stambha*, the primal pillar. More about columns in my next mail.

Columns were very common in ancient Greece where they were used in many of the temples and buildings and had a sacred connection. However when the Romans took over their style of architecture and created columns they were mostly decorative. The Corinthian column in particular comes to mind which has a decorative upper end. Columns for us have a hoary history and meaning. The first column was called the Indra *stambha* and planted by Indra to separate the water from the sky to create a space for human habitation and this is the paradigm for all *stambhas* that follow. The Indra *stambha* in the ultimate analysis is a metaphor for the space between the subject and the object, where knowledge arises and is therefore an image of *jnana* or knowledge. Then there are *mandapa stambhas,* pillars, in a pavilion where they create a beautiful space that replicates the cosmic space, victory *stambhas,* vistory pillars, planted by kings, a *stambha* to proclaim Buddhism planted by Ashoka, the *kalpavriksha,* a wish fulfilling tree, which becomes a natural *stambha* going from the netherworld to the sky. When we sit under a tree it becomes a beautifully cosmic moment and is conducive to both *satya* and *saundarya,* truth and beauty. How different are the meanings of pillars in the East and the West.

An interesting distinction between the Western and Indian way of thinking and feeling is seen in the development of the image of the Buddha. One of the earliest images of the Buddha were to come from Gandhara, the present day Afghanistan. The Buddha there was represented as a person of power, muscular and standing upright, almost like a soldier, with a stern face. This early image of the Buddha was not acceptable to the Indian psyche. They were looking for an image that would speak of Buddha's gentle smile, his inward search for peace, sitting in the yogic position and showing what are called *mahapurusha lakshana* or the 32 marks of a great person. They were to get this in what is called the Mathura Buddha. The Indian psyche, as opposed to the Western mentality, prefers the inward peace rather than outward power, gentleness rather than brute strength, love and sweet persuasion rather than edicts and laws.

When one is buying a home or refurbishing it, there are a lot of Interior Designers and Decorators both in New York and in Mumbai. Whether tastefully or garishly done these designers decorate homes and create beautiful living spaces for us. Whether it is paint or lighting, drapes or carpets, they certainly do a wonderful job and we then enjoy our homes. The concept of adorning one's home is very different in traditional India and one sees this even today in rural, more than, urban homes. Adornment for us is always for someone other and higher than us. Adorning and beautifying our home is not so much for us but for the indwelling sprit of the home. The motifs and designs, the *akriti* and the *rachana,* forms and patterns, of these adornments are also very different. Generally, they are taken from archetypal symbols like the lotus and the tree, the sun and the moon, creepers and birds. These confer on the home a certain sacredness, they protect the inhabitants and ensure that we in our daily life never lose sight of a reality beyond and above our present reality. Our homes are a gift and a blessing to us and not just a property that we have acquired monetarily (and keep on paying monthly for it!).

Talking of adornment let me tell you about the traditional concept of a woman's adornment. A woman, traditionally adorns herself with the 16 adornments from head to toe, with ornaments, unguents, flowers and clothes. She does this not just to beautify herself but for the eyes of her beloved, whether it is her lover, husband or god. Her adornment is an offering, her gift to someone she loves. I can already see feminists raising their eye brows and whispering, "I adorn for myself and not for anyone else". In the Indian tradition we constantly move away from *ahankara,* to *asmita*, egoism to enlightened self-awareness. *Ahamkara* is aggressive self-identification, while *asmita* is refined self-awareness. There is a fundamental difference between the two. *Ahamkara* or one's personal ego will be troublesome in the long run, it might offend others and at the end of the day may let you down. *Asmita* or refined self-awareness takes your attention from the outer and superficial, from personal aggrandizement to something deeper and long lasting. Adornment in the latter sense is an offering, a sacrificee and not self-serving. Would women in the Western world accept this?

शाखा डाक घर
BRANCH POST OFFICE
स. ७ तै १०

The Hindu civilisation started on a joyous note. Our *rishis*, or first seers, were poets of beauty, they were wonderstruck by the beauty of the universe around them and mankind's place in it, and they expressed this in joyous poetry or Vedic hymns. Suffering in the Vedas was caused by the loss of knowledge which they referred to as stealing of cows. Over the centuries this was to change and today the recognition and redress of social realities and injustice is the watch word of politicians and our gurus and then passed on to us. But for those of us who are able to cut through painful social realities there is the fountainhead of joy and beauty to be discovered. We do not have to listen to messengers or sons of gods, no commandments or edicts, no original sin to worry about. A Hindu is closest to his god, in whichever way he conceives him or her, is when he is in a state of *ananda* or joyous and blissful. Nay, at that moment he is god himself.

गांधी शताब्दी 1869-1969
GANDHI CENTENARY
पोस्ट कार्ड
POST CARD
केवल पता
ADDRESS ONLY
भारत
INDIA
GANDHI CENTENARY
ALLAHABAD H.O.

When one is confronted by two opposing thoughts we have three options: leaving them separate and in opposition, synthesis where we combine the two into one but in doing so they lose their unique identity, and in syncreticism where we bring the two together but ensure that they maintain their individual identity. The first two, I call, the Western way of handling the problem, while syncretism is uniquely a Hindu solution. When we apply syncretism to matters religious or philosophic, that is where the Hindu genius comes in. A striking example of this is the image of the Ardhanarishvara, a syncretic coming together of Shiva and Parvati. While each of them maintain their identity, they create a biune unity, one complementing the other, and the two together creating a new and beautiful reality. Another significant image is that of Harihara, a syncretic coming together of Shiva and Vishnu. Syncretism suggests inclusion and not negation, enlarging the original concept rather than diminishing or changing it. Syncretism is another way in which the Hindu mind is pluralistic, unlike the Western monolithic mind.

If one were to ask, "How do you make something that is half, into full?" a common answer would be "double the half and it becomes full". While this may be rationally and mathematically correct, it is not philosophically correct for the Indian mind. A half truth cannot become the full truth by doubling it, rather a half truth or *ardhya satya*, becomes the full truth by combing it with its opposite half. Thus, while day is a half truth, but it becomes the full truth only when it is combined with night. In bringing together two opposing truths one is defining totality. The rational mind delights in half truths, the Indian philosophic mind celebrates the full truth or *purna satya*. It is only *purna satya* that can lay claim to be transcendent and approach ultimate reality. The *ardha satyas* of the modern West remain at best material or psychological truths.

The modern Western civilization is sustained and inspired by the concept of the Absolute. The Absolute for it is perfect, ultimate, monochromatic, a position not open to any questioning. We see this not only in Abrahamic theology but in their social functioning as well. Strict adherence to the law, rigid social behavior, borders and fences around properties, a closed door to one's home and many more. The Hindu tradition on the other hand steers away from the Absolute and prefers a negotiable, contextual higher authority. Not one concept of the truth, but multiple; not monochromatic but polychromatic, not one God, but many gods, not one, but plural, not one language, but many, not binary divisions but a seamless movement from one to the other. It is this pluralism in thought and behaviour, customs and cuisine, that defines the Hindu tradition and because of this, it is open to all and does not accept the Abrahamic Absolute. It is very difficult explaining this to the modern Western person. The Orientalists of the 19th century denigrated our country on this very point calling our gods as monsters and our thinking as uncivilized.

Philately: King Of Hobbies
COLLECT
INDIA POSTAGE STAMPS
CONTACT
Nearest Philatelic Bureau
भारत INDIA
50
महात्मा गाँधी MAHATMA GANDHI
POST CARD
प्र.पु./SPP/HYD - 2021 पोस्ट कार्ड
पिन PIN
(इस लाइन के नीचे न तो लिखें और न ही मुद्रित करें Do not write or print below this line)

The word art is a Western word and although we use it commonly in India as well it creates problems. There is no simple definition of the word art but perhaps this, "Art is the creation of beautiful objects", might suffice. This Western word art brings with it baggage like high art and low art, expensive and cheap, as also art markets where art is judged by the price it gets. Recently a new gallery was added to our Mumbai museum and it was called; "A Gallery of Buddhist Art". It sent chills down my spine. Buddha would have been horrified to see this. This gallery should have been called Celebrating The Buddha and Buddhism. Unfortunately the modern Western mind cannot get away from art and art history.

Once, Vijay and Suresh were in an animated conversation in Ottawa, while the two of them and my friend John, the four of us were sipping coffee at Starbucks on a nice spring day. During the conversation Vijay asked Suresh, "How is mother"? Suresh gave a lengthy answer describing his mother's medical problems but then assured us that she was on the mend. After Vijay and Suresh left, John and I lingered and then John said, "You Indians do not know how to use pronouns." "How so?" I asked. Vijay should have said, "How is your mother and not just mother". To which I said, "To us Indians, your mother is also my mother and therefore we do not use pronouns. We leave all the pronouns for you Canadians!"

Most people equate religion with god and the practice of religion with institutions like temple, church, mosque, synagogue, *gurudwara* or fire temple. However did you know that the Hindu tradition is the only wisdom tradition in the world that lets you be a Hindu without believing in god? We Hindus spell god with a lower case g and not a capital G. While all other religions insist that God is the truth, we Hindus say that truth is god. And that truth for the Hindus is not monolithic or monochromatic but polychromatic and pluralistic. The Vedas have said that, *ekam sat bahudha vipra vadanti*, truth is one but the wise speak about it in many different ways. There are many outcomes of this Hindu position which I will write in my next postcard.

CANADA-NEW ZEALAND
Denmark, Italy, Poland, Germany, Netherlands, Spain,
Sweden, France, Dubai, Oman, Bahrin, Saudi Arabia,
Singapore, Hong Kong, Malaysia, South Africa, Kenya,
GPO PINCODE
NO CLEARANCE ON SUNDAY
INDIA POST

The theologically minded Hindus have many Gods to choose from and engage in their prescribed practices and rituals and derive faith and sustenance from it, and rightly so. This is their chosen spiritual path and no one has a right to denigrate it. However equally there are non-theistic paths available to Hindus and these are mainly two: abstract contemplation or what is called meditation and aesthetic contemplation which in Sanskrit is called *rasa svadana*. A prepared and trained aesthete can reach the same level of higher awareness (consciousness) that a religious person can attain. That truth of the aesthete is also sometimes called poetic truth and best be known by the trinity, *satyam*, *sundaram*, *smaranam*, truth-beauty-remembrance. This remembrance is of who we really are at our innermost self, also called *atman*. In not putting down any approaches to higher realisation I am very proud that the Hindu tradition gives us this non-theistic option.

I was once speaking with the late Syed Haider Raza, a prominent 20th century painter from India. As our conversation proceeded to discuss the finer points of Indian painting he said, "Do you see any straight lines in nature?". "No", I said, "but why do you ask?" The Indian mind, he said, is a reflection of the world around us, of our majestic trees, beautiful blossoms, billowing clouds and whispering rivers. It is like that curved and dancing line, moving and spiralling, twisting and turning, meandering and winding . It is driven and inspired by emotion and feeling, desire and the search for beauty. The Western mind is generally driven by reason and rationality, intellectuality and ratiocination, and can be best be understood by straight lines The Indian mind quickly transforms what it sees with its two eyes through the third eye into metaphors of beauty. Art or our expression of beauty is a window of our civilsation and is therefore a useful tool to compare different civilizations.

Sitting in the Willingdon Club in Mumbai I overhear parents talking to their little children in English and this led to a series of questions in my mind. The sociology of this phenomenon is quite obvious. Urban Indians have not been able, or do not want to, shake off their colonial past and want to hang on to many of their trappings. The English language is important to them and is an assurance that they and their children, will be a part of a larger world. At one level I am prepared to understand this and even accept it. But do they realise the price they are paying for it? With English alone they will not be able to access, understand and celebrate the Indian civilisation. English as a language just does not have the words, the grammar and the syntax to uncover the many beautiful layers of our culture. If I point this out to them, and they turn around and tell me, that they are not interested in understanding our culture and civilisation, all I would say to them, is that they will be the poorer for it. The same thing applies to second generation children of the Indian diaspora.

The noted music conductor Zubin Mehta once said, (paraphrased): if a civilisation has the same word for yesterday and tomorrow, it must be deeply thoughtful. Yes indeed, Mr.Mehta. We use the word *kal* for both yesterday and tomorrow, not because we do not have adequate words. Actually, in Gujarati we do say *gai kal* for yesterday and *avti kal* for tomorrow. But in using the same word we are making a statement of our concept of time which is circular and spiral and not linear. Mircea Eliade called the Indian sense of time sacred and the Western view of time as profane The Indian view of time gives us a vaster notion of time and even leads to timelessness. Whereas the Western view of time being linear leads to a binary, fragmented view of the world. The former leads to concepts of a past and future birth, whereas the latter view restricts our life to only one birth. The Western view inevitably, though rational, misses the many beautiful mystical views of the world which we in India revel in.

भारतीय डाक
India Post
ଚିଠି ଓ ପାର୍ସଲ
पत्र एवं पार्सल
ମନି ଅର୍ଡର
मनी आर्डर
ସ୍ପିଡ୍ ପୋଷ୍ଟ
स्पीड पोस्ट
ବ୍ୟବସାୟିକ ଡାକ
बिजनेस पोस्ट
ଏକ୍ସପ୍ରେସ ପାର୍ସଲ ପୋଷ୍ଟ
एक्सप्रेस पार्सल पोस्ट
ଡାକଘର ସଞ୍ଚୟ ଜମା
डाकघर बचत बैंक

In a recent World Bank Happiness Report India was ranked 126 out of 137 countries. The world at large, and even some Indians, consider this as a holy document. The criteria that this report uses are: per capta income, presence of charitable organisations, corruption, social welfare benefits and a sense of individual independence and freedom. Instead we in India measure happiness by how we celebrate our religious festivals, how often the family eats together, how often do grandparents get to see their grandchildren, how often do people go to see a doctor or ask advice for depression or loneliness, how often do you have a cup of tea with your neighbours, do you have to make an appointment to see your friend, do you have a good night's sleep without taking any pills. I submit, if the World Bank uses these criteria India would come out much higher.

In times modern one's self-image is determined to a large extent by politicians and economists. In Canada where I have spent more than 50 years of my life I have had to reluctantly submit to its socialistic culture and politics. This creates a flat egalitarian society with a number of social benefits for its population, but in doing so it blurs individual identity. In traditional India, and much of India is still traditional, the civilisation and culture is feudal and hence it provides a hierarchy of many sorts. In India I can therefore craft my own self-image, be it religious, cultural or aesthetic, without societal pressure. Since the social norms in India are wide, I can walk on the street in my pyjamas or proper clothes. In India I do not have to explain who I am, as my image speaks for itself and I get the appropriate response from society. In Canada, this is not so for me. Therefore, you have to decide what your self-image is and then determine what is home for you. Remember you can change a lot of things about your image but not the colour of your skin.

He was a 53 year old Professor of Indian origin, self-absorbed and egoistic, and announced himself as shaped by the Western civilization. Gift giving is an important part of this Western civilisation: Christmas, Mother's Day, Father's Day, Birthdays, Anniversaries are some examples. The culture of gifts is important in this civilisation and very often defines your relationship with the other. These days gifts are often store bought and gift wrapped by the store clerk: shiny paper, bow and a bag with tissue paper, sometimes with flowers. Sadly our Professor however knew only these kind of gifts and since he did not get any of this he felt that he was not welcome. Did he know that, we in India have our gifts stored in our heart and not bought from a store: gifts like enduring love, deep concern, constant wishes for well being, sincere desire for success, that the winds be always on his back and that the road ahead be easy, a homemade simple meal. These and other prayers and thoughts, are precious and not conveyed by well wrapped gifts, but by words or gestures or sometimes by a simple holding of hands or a look in the eyes. Indian gifts do not always have a gift wrap. Wish the Professor knew.

ಚಾಮುಂಡಿ ಬೆಟ್ಟ ಶಾಖಾ ಅಂಚೆ ಕಛೇರಿ
ವ್ಯವಹಾರದ ಸಮಯ
ಬೆಳಗ್ಗೆ 09.00 ಗಂಟೆ ಯಿಂದ
ಮಧ್ಯಾಹ್ನ 02.00 ಗಂಟೆ ವರೆಗೆ
ಭಾನುವಾರ ರಜೆ
WORKING HOURS
09:00 am to 02:00pm
SUNDAY HOLIDAY
570010

The sacred for us in the Indian civilisation came first, then the divine and we make no difference between the sacred and the secular for they are a continuum. The earth and the wind, the sun and the moon, the rivers and the lakes were all sacred to the Vedic *rishis*. The concept of the sacred for the Indian mind went beyond that to everyday objects: your home, your kitchen, your parents, your parent's or guru's feet, your language, your books and so on. Pilgrimages were to sacred spots and visiting your parents in their home, or visiting an ancestral home, was also a pilgrimage of sorts. We believe that the spirit of a person lives in their home, or cremation site or grave, even if the person has moved away. Today, even in India this concept is fading and the sacred is being replaced by what is comfortable and convenient. All of this has a Western colour to it for in the West only the gods and perhaps the human life are sacred, but not the objects of a human being especially an elder. When nothing is sacred, other than matters religious, it will lead to a very impoverished mind. In upholding the sacred we in India bring sacredness, meaning and richness to our lives.

Gandhi, among others, was a staunch critic of Western Modernity. He once wrote: 'So understanding and so believing, it behooves every lover of India to cling to the old Indian civilization even as a child clings to the mother's breast'. My own position is a bit different. I feel that we should accept Western modernisation, learn from it and improve our country in its socio-economic limitations, without accepting the Western concept of modernity which is godless secularism. We in India need Western technology, we must remain devotees in the temples of science in the West, but that is where we should stop. Our gods, our mythology, our mystical thinking, our traditions must not play second fiddle to the modern West. For that, is our strength, our heritage.

The celebration of the individual is never a Hindu ideal, rather the fullness of humanity is what the tradition upholds. For the Hindu, it is the family, the community, the village, the country and the universe in that order. The individual as an entity is always downplayed, rather the individual for the Hindu, is a part of a larger whole. The limited 'I" dissolves into the larger 'we'. Take the way we construct our names as an example. In some parts of India our name is in three parts: our proper name, our father's name and surname. In the south our name starts with the name of our village or community. A wedding invitation has names of family members, past and present. In many parts of India the system of a joint family still exists where the head of the family is the grandfather or even the great grandfather. In the modern Western civilisation we celebrate the individual and individuality. This leads to nuclear families and children asserting their individuality as early as age 16 or 18. Both systems have their own strengths but the traditional Indian system creates holistic families and communities. Whereas the Western individualistic and nuclear family system ultimately leads to loneliness and alienation.

Jawaharlal Nehru, our first prime minister, wrote in his Discovery of India, that "India is a bundle of contradictions held together by invisible threads." That is a very apt statement by a Western mind, which is what Nehru had. It is Indian pluralism, which the West calls contradictions and those threads are the silken threads of love and understanding and tolerance and acceptance. Ours, unlike the West, is not a monolithic, monotheistic, monochromatic civilisation. Our civilization was born and grew in a lush tropical country, where between the earth and the sky, there was a plethora of fecund and luxuriant vegetation: trees, flowers, fruits, rivers, birds, all very beautiful and each individual a part of the larger whole. This applies to our languages, our customs, our traditions and our religions. That is why we are uncomfortable with a monochromatic, monotheistic world.

The word *ananda* is central to the Indian world view and has many shades of meanings, but is hard to translate. Bliss, joyous equanimity, serenity are some of its limited meanings in English. *Ananda*, for us, is a state of being, above pleasure and happiness, it is a state where we have accepted both pleasure and pain as part of our life but reside in a plane higher than that. It is a place of stillness of thought, of the body and mind, a state where there are no questions, but a supreme state of being above the dichotomies and binaries of life. This state of the mind can be reached by meditation, either abstract or aesthetic. Western traditions do recognise states such as peace and bliss. However there is one big difference, *ananda* for us is a part of *brahmajnana* or transcendent knowledge, when we are in a state of *ananda* we are very close to our true self. Whereas, I do not think, the West can raise their concept of peace and serenity to a level higher than that.

2004
भारत INDIA
1854
500
भारतीय डाक के 150 वर्ष 150 YEARS OF INDIA POST
AIR MAIL
2004
भारत INDIA
500
भारतीय डाक के 150 वर्ष 150 YEARS OF INDIA POST
2004
भारत INDIA
500
भारतीय डाक के 150 वर्ष 150 YEARS OF INDIA POST
2004
भारत INDIA
e.post
SPEED POST
MEDIA POST
500
भारतीय डाक के 150 वर्ष 150 YEARS OF INDIA POST
1854
2004
HALF ANNA
वर्ष YEARS
150
भारतीय डाक INDIA POST

Very often in Indic thought we use the word inner, as in inner self, inner mind and finally of course *atman*, the innermost mind. What is this inner and outer that we are referring to? Ultimately you will say the mind is only one. Let me quote a line from Tagore: "With the light of my eyes I behold the world. When however there is no light (that is with eyes closed) I behold the world within." When you engage with the world with your two eyes you are using the faculty of *buddhi* and *anumana*, intellect and inference. This gives you only a limited view of the world. When however, you transcend the intellect, you enter the mystical spaces of your mind, an aesthetic space, above and beyond the limited rational mind, where there is no fragmentation, no binaries, where space is vast and time is eternal. This inner mind or the *atman* is a very Indian view of life. The modern Western mind may talk of a soul but that does not come close to our concept of the *atman*.

The modern Western civilization is driven by three forces: Science and Technology, Fabian Socialism and Christianity. The main thrust of this, as I understand it, is social justice and equality. Having lived in Great Britain and Canada, I feel, noble though it is, this has failed. Despite its best efforts it has not been able to create a just and egalitarian society. I feel that fundamentally the premise of equality is faulty and at best a political jargon. The world was never equal, nor can it made so. On the other hand, we in the Indian civilization, recognised that the world is unequal and unjust in many ways. Ours is a hierarchical and stratified society, where while accepting inequality we do strive to redress as much injustice as we can. But the Hindu mind, is a feudal mind and is quite comfortable with hierarchies of different sorts. While in today's India we do see aspirations and the desire to ascend the social ladder but this is not widespread. We have the wisdom to try and improve our lot in life but also accept the situation we are in.

A common phrase in India is, “please adjust”. You enter an over crowded compartment in a train and say, “please adjust” and indeed somehow a seat becomes available, when there was none. I am having a busy day a the office and an Indian patient comes on the wrong day of his appointment and tells the receptionist, “please adjust”, and we do. The contractor who is two weeks behind in his work says, “please adjust” and we do, with some annoyance. The tailor who promised to bring the clothes on Monday does not show up till Saturday and says with a smile, “please adjust”. What choice do we have! I am not condoning bad social and work ethics, but being able to accept with a smiling face, that everything in life does not work like clock work, or we do not insist that a bench with four seats can accommodate only four, goes a long way in creating peace of mind and even making new friends when you are the sixth person on that bench!

TRAVELS
फ्लोटिंग पोस्ट ऑफ़िस
فلوٹنگ پوسٹ آفس
FLOATING POST OFFICE NEHRU PARK (PIN 190001)

Let me relate to you a story. Two friends went for lunch at their favourite restaurant. The food and service were good and the conversation was congenial. When it came to paying the bill there was the usual tussle, each trying to outdo the other to pay the bill. A Buddhist monk was sitting on the next table and he intervened. "May I suggest a solution?" Pointing to me he said, "You pay for your friend's lunch and your friend will pay for yours." I was struck with this simple solution. Both of us get a free lunch." This was Zen Buddhism at its best. Which underlines an essential truth that when I pay for my own lunch, and my friend for his, we each get satisfaction of being materially independent. It pampers our ego. When however, I pay for his lunch, I have the pleasure of having done a kind act. He in turn gets the same satisfaction. While the restaurant gets its bill paid, but the way in which it is paid, leaves a beautiful feeling for my friend and myself. Small acts of love and compassion are features of an enlightened mind, which is what all Hindus should cultivate.

When you live in India you get your religion and philosophy by osmosis: on the street, in a store, under a tree sipping tea, from a taxi driver, from family elders, even the chap who stands with a green and red flag at a village railway crossing. I have been privy to all of this and more. Every so often people will join both hands and lift them up to the sky and say, "He will decide". When things don't work out an elder will say, "Don't fret, God knows best." An old uncle will recite a verse from the Gita, "Do your duty and do not expect any rewards.' "Ram! Ram! Or Jai Shri Krishna! Or Jai Jinendra! are common greetings. When you are bemoaning a bad outcome, someone reminds you, don't blame yourself, it is a result of your *karma* from your past birth. Traditionally most of our first names were from the religious tradition that we belonged to. Therefore if you were a Vaishnava most of the names would be that of Vishnu, so that when you call that person, you are also remembering Vishnu. Many are the ways in which we blend religion and philosophy in our daily living. Something you do not commonly find in the modern West.

Let me give you a few more examples how our character is molded by osmosis and not only by our scriptures. Let us take body language to start with. Quite often when asked about our well being we fold our hands and point them to the sky as if to say, "God looks after me." Very often when we enter our offices we would bow down and touch the ground, as if to offer salutations to mother earth. A musician when he steps on the stage would do something similar as if to ask for the blessings of the stage for the success of the performance. When you enter someone's home and say "what a beautiful home" the owner of the home might say, "it is because of blessings from my elders and you that I have acquired this home." When a reader compliments you on your book the author would often say, "I did not write this book. It was written through me." When a visitor leaves our home we say something like, "Come again" or "May God be with you till we meet again". There are numerous ways in which we bring God into our daily lives, not by religious rites or rituals, but by simple acts of veneration. This is refreshingly different from what I have observed in Canada.

Most civilisations have sacred trees: Christmas Tree of Europe, Bau Bau Tree of Portugal, Cedar Tree of Persia, Cherry Tree of Japan and so on. We in India, have our sacred Ashwatha or Pipal Tree. However there is one big difference in our Tree. The Gita refers to life as an upside down Pipal tree with its roots above and branches below. The reference here, is that for us, the source of our life comes from the heaven above, that is our roots are spiritual and not earthy or material. This defines our world view. While we live on this earth and material quests occupy our quotidian minds, but we never forget that our ultimate quest has to be *moksha* or spiritual freedom. This *moksha* is not just a far away ideal, or something we achieve in our after life, but it is *jivan mukti* that we strive for, spiritual joy and freedom in this very life. The modern West with its emphasis on "life, liberty and happiness" needs to take a page from our book.

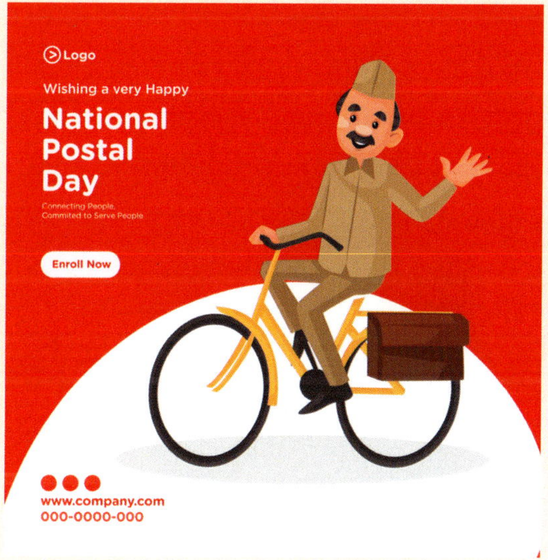

Of the three Western countries I have lived in, Canada is the youngest and compared to India, where our recorded history goes back 5000 years, it is still in its infancy. In an ancient country like India, it is not at all uncommon to see ancient buildings and monuments that are several hundred years old. The Bau Bau tree in our Mumbai Museum is about 300 years old, so are many Banayan trees across the country. I have in my collection paintings that go back to the 16th century. Wandering through antique shops in Mumbai's Chor Bazar (Robber's Market) there are artefacts lying around which are easily hundreds of years old. I must admit that I get a sense of security and stability in the company of old monuments and objects, it is as if I am standing next to some elder in the family. I say to myself, that if a particular structure or organisation has survived this long then it will continue to exist for several hundred years more. Old is gold as they say, but anything old is also a statement of the longevity of the civiisation, an assurance that it has withstood hazards and perils, and likewise, I would do the same. I miss this feeling walking around the modern streets or parks or shiny steel and glass buildings of Canada.

One day I had invited a friend from Washington, D.C. for lunch at our club in Mumbai. We had settled down to a nice pre-lunch conversation, when his wife came running in, apologizing for being late. Showing off her new purchase she said, "Looking at my new Indian jacket". I looked at it and said, "Joan, it is made in India, but it is not Indian." She did not quite understand and this started a beautiful inquiry in my mind. I realised that not everything made in India is Indian, for that matter not every Indian is an Indian, by some standards. That is when the phrase "Akriti to Sanskriti" arose in my mind and this resulted in a book. All our decorative forms, motifs, designs (subsumed under the umbrella term *akriti*) stem from an underlying Indian *sanskriti* (culture). In the case of Joan's jacket, the pastel green colour is not Indian, for we use bright colours and each colour means something different. Further, cut flowers as a design are never Indian, for us it is a garland or a meandering vine that is Indian, reminding us that fragmentation goes against the Indian world view. For a Western mind anything bought in India is Indian, not for me. I suggest many NRIs should wear a T-shirt that says, "Made in India. Export Quality"!

The previous postcard raised some troubling questions. Who is to decide what and who is an Indian, what are the markers of something Indian? Without attempting to define that, there is one observation that is worth making. Until the European colonisers came to India, we accommodated and assimilated most people who came to India. I am not overlooking the tension between the Muslims and the Hindus particularly from the time of Aurangzeb. Aesthetically, but not theologically, there was one unified Indian culture. The Muslims contributed richly to our cuisine and costume, music and dance, architecture and painting. However it were the Anglo-Saxon Britishers who not only colonised our country but our minds. There was something about their culture which an ordinary Indian could not understand or assimilate and vice versa. They looted our country. With the advent of globilisation arose the globalized Indian. More about that in my next mail.

In the last decade or two we have seen the rise of the Globalized Indian, who is comfortable with pasta and *paratha*, New York and Nagpur, Coke and Coconut water. That globalized Indian is particularly seen in metropolitan India and not in rural India, which sets up that divide between rural and urban. Globalisation in trade led to the globilasation of our culture: music, cuisine, costume. All to the good so far. My problem is, what are the metaphysical roots of that globalized Indian, does he or she subscribe to traditional Indian culture and values, would he long for India if he migrates to the modern West? I do not have the answers to these existential questions, nor do I want to proseletyse. As far as I am concerned, after living in the modern West for more than half a century, and even though I have imbibed some of its values and habits, I would prefer to return to India, and end my life as a true Indian, and not as a person of Indian origin. I have lived too under a Oak tree, I want to be nourished by the roots of the Pipal tree.

Philately: King Of Hobbies
COLLECT
INDIA POSTAGE STAMPS
CONTACT
Nearest Philatelic Bureau
भारत INDIA
50
महात्मा गाँधी MAHATMA GANDHI
प्र.मु./SPP/HYD - 2021 पोस्ट कार्ड POST CARD
पिन PIN
(इस लाइन के नीचे न तो लिखें और न ही मुद्रित करें Do not write or print below this line)

There is widespread existential despair, loneliness and suffering in the Western modern project. It cannot turn around to its medieval roots committed, as it is to technology and intellectuality. like Lucky's wordless speech in Waiting for Godot, or the final scream in Bergman's *Cries and Whispers*, the modern Western person can only express its anguished cry. Like a tethered beast it grunts and growls, looking at its toys, which are no longer able to elevate him but can only make endless patterns within its own petty boundaries. "What else do we have," it cries out in anguish, "But reason?" Such a query can only be answered in silence lest the attempted answer drag one back into the blighted circle of reason and intellect.

After you have read all my postcards you might wonder, that for me, the Indian civilization is perfect and devoid of fault lines. No, that is not so. We in India have a fair share of structural social and economic problems. Let me list a few: the pernicious caste system, unabashed patriarchy, unbridled unethical practices and disrespect for social ethics, a preference for individual salvation rather than the salvation of the community, inter and intra-religious conflicts and more. Even though I accept this as a blot on our civilization, you might ask, why is that I feel, that at the end of the day the Indian civilization is superior to its Western counterpart. I will answer that in my next mail.

Despite all these problems and more, ours is a joyous civilization, where we celebrate life with zest and gusto, where each of us is guaranteed perfect knowledge, if not in this birth then in future births, where poverty is not understood as suffering, where our social fabric is robust so that we are closely connected to each other in the web of life, and because of this, feelings of loneliness and alienation are very uncommon, where the creation of what is beautiful is an integral part of life and our homes and temples are a repository of beauty, where we use colours with abandon, where religion is not divorced from life, where we find unity in diversity and pluralism is our watchword, where the sacred and the secular are a continuum and where truth is god and not God, truth, where the aroma of the earth pervades all aspects of our life and even while raising our arms up to the sky we stand firmly on the ground, where the colors of the sky are also those of our mind, and thus we connect the earth with the sky, where we live our quotidian life with linear time but our mind functions in circular time, and infinity is not just an empty concept, but part of our daily and artistic vocabulary, where our view of the world is vast and not limited.

भारतीय डाक
India Post
भारतीय डाक
INDIA POST
दार्जीलिङ
DARJEELING
734 101
"Speed Post booking
is done here"
WESTERN
UNION

The world has been Eurocentric for the last few centuries. But the needle is pointing undeniably Eastward. Regrettably in looking for our place in the Eurocentric world order, we allow ourselves to get Westernized and globalized. We ignore our enduring values because today's India is poor, backward, third world and so on. However, let us not forget that it is mainly because of our colonizers that we are economically backward today. Wherever you live, it is time for you to stand up for the Indian civilization, to convey to the world that ours is an ancient but living and beautiful civilization. We have to respond to the West, not by defending our values and culture, but by asserting them.

डाकघर
POST OFFICE
इंडिया पोस्ट पेमेंट्स बैंक
हिक्किम शाखा डाकघर
हिक्किम
HIKKIM
172114
भारतीय डाक
India Post
"विश्व का सबसे ऊँचाई पर स्थित डाकघर"
"THE WORLD'S HIGHEST POST OFFICE"
HEIGHT ऊँचाई 4440 Mtr. मी. {14567 Ft. फीट}

So, as I end, what am I asking you to do? I am not asking you to give up or change your life, your ambitions, your dreams in any significant way. However, I do ask that when you have a quiet and contemplative moment, that you think about the fault lines of the modern Western civilization in which you live, the strengths of the Indian civilization, its enduring values and lofty metaphysical ideas, and see if even some of it can be made a part of your living life. Aristotle once said, "You should entertain every thought even if you do not agree with it." Your life, wherever you live, will only be richer with Indian values and ideals.